Affiliate Marketing

A Proven Step by Step Guide for Beginners to Learn All the Secrets to Make Money Online Using Paid Advertising from Low Ticket to High Ticket Programs!

Michael Robert Fortunate

Table of Contents

Introduction

Congratulations on purchasing *Affiliate Marketing: A Proven Step by Step Guide for Beginners to Learn All the Secrets to Make Money Online Using Paid Advertising from Low Ticket to High Ticket Programs!*

Marketing has taken different faces in today's world but affiliate marketing is still one of the most hyped ones. There are countless success stories about affiliate marketing that you will find on the internet. Every internet marketer in today's world aspires to generate a sustainable and regular flow of income but can affiliate marketing provide you that? The answer is yes but there are some conditions attached to it.

Firstly, you need to have a well-structured business plan that will guide you in the right way. For this, you need to fully understand the dynamics of the world of affiliate marketing and have all of it under your grasp. Secondly, you also need to know how you can leverage the influence of social media in order to drive in more sales and thus, bring home more profits. And that is exactly what is covered in this book.

The aim of this book is not only to provide you with a comprehensive guide on how affiliate marketing works but also to educate you on all the key factors that are necessary to keep in mind while framing a successful affiliate marketing program.

With this book, you will become a pro at the various strategies of paid advertising from both low ticket and high ticket programs.

Every effort was put into compiling this book so that it can serve fruitful to every aspiring affiliate marketer.

Chapter 1: Why Affiliate Marketing Is the Best Way To Start Off Your Internet Business?

Do you dream of making some sustainable passive income? Imagine a day where you can make money while you are still asleep in bed! Sound great, doesn't it? Well, it is easier said than done. You will need a solid plan in order to move forward with affiliate marketing and build a stable career with it.

But first, you must have a clear idea about what affiliate marketing really is. The main idea of affiliate marketing is solely based on revenue sharing. The idea is that when you are promoting a product, which actually belongs to someone else, over an affiliate marketing network and someone ends up buying that particular product, you will earn a commission. Simply put, you will get an incentive every time someone buys a product that you have promoted.

But to break it down to the basic level, affiliate marketing has four different parties involved in it and each one of them has been explained below.

- **The Merchant:** The merchant can be anyone who is responsible for the creation of the product that you are promoting. It can be a brand, an individual, a vendor, a seller or even a retailer. It can be a content creator selling online courses about photography or it can be a big brand like Mitsubishi manufacturing air conditioners. An affiliate marketing program can have anyone as its merchant starting from solo entrepreneurs to the biggest companies there is. But the merchant does not require active participation. All it has to do is possess a product that can be sold.

- **The Affiliate:** Also referred to as the publisher, the affiliate too is not limited to any specific entity. It can be a company or it can also be an individual. The affiliate is the person who is responsible for the promotion of the products. He/she can promote as many products as they want but their responsibility lies in acquiring the attention of potential customers and convincing them to buy the product. This is mostly done through the establishment of a review blog which the customers can read and end up buying products they like.

- **The Consumer:** The consumer definitely holds an important position in the entire cycle of affiliate marketing. This is because the concept of sustainability resides on the fact that there are some actual sales and without consumers, there will be no sales. So, there will be no commissions and no one will make any profit. The affiliate approaches the potential consumer through various methods. It can be done through social media, a blog or even through digital billboards. But whether or not the consumer is made aware of the fact that the product is part of an affiliate marketing system lies entirely in the hands of the affiliate. But since these days, transparent affiliate marketing is being encouraged and it is also one of the strategies for gaining the trust of the consumers, the affiliates usually choose to let the consumers know. Despite the product being a part of an affiliate marketing system, the consumer is not charged anything extra.

- **The Network:** This is the fourth component of affiliate marketing. Although the network is not always considered as a component by everyone, it should be. This is because the network is what serves as the intermediary between the merchant and the affiliate. But the presence of a network is not something mandatory.

You can promote someone's product directly and develop a direct arrangement with the merchant regarding your share. But in some cases, in order to be able eligible to work as an affiliate for a certain merchant, going through a network is mandatory. In that scenario, the network also acts as a database apart from being the intermediary. Currently, the biggest affiliate network is owned by Amazon. With them, anyone can become an affiliate by signing up and then they will be given a custom affiliate link. The affiliate will earn a small commission every time someone buys a product through his/her custom affiliate link.

So, affiliate marketing is one of the best sources of passive income and also perfect for starting your online business. All you need to know is how you can drive more traffic and also use effective strategies to convince the customers regarding the potential that each of the products have. Only then can you make some meaningful income out of it.

If you are feeling confused and thinking that it is too much to take in then don't worry as this book will make all of it seem way easier. And this chapter is all about why you should choose affiliate marketing at all when it comes to starting your own business online.

Here are some reasons why you should start affiliate marketing today!

Reason 1 – It is Quite Affordable to Start

Of course, a start-up might seem all fancy but have you considered the costs associated with it? In most cases, it is huge and requires a lot of funding. On the other hand, starting an affiliate marketing business requires a meager amount of investment as compared to the other modes of online business. The best thing is that most of the affiliate programs that you will find on the internet are all free to join. Moreover, the product that you are actually promoting is manufactured by someone else and so you need not worry about that cost as well. So, there are practically no start-up costs associated. All you need to do is adapt some effective monetization methods on your own website. All you need to invest in is for setting up your own website. You will have to pay for your website domain and hosting services.

Reason 2 – You Will Get an Assured Commission

There are definitely a lot of ways in which you can earn money online but do all of them reap 100% guaranteed profits? No. But with affiliate marketing, with every sale you make, you will get an assured amount of commission. No one can take that away from you. It is completely genuine. But you do need to come up with some quality content that will grab the customer's attention and make them want to buy the product thus resulting in sales.

Reason 3 – There is an Endless Amount of Professional Independence

One of the best aspects of doing approaching affiliate marketing as your online business is that you will be your own boss. There will be no one to tell you what you should do or how you should do it. Everything will lie in your own hands. You can decide the hours you want to work for and you can even work from any location in the world. The only thing you would need is a stable internet connection and you are good to go! Every poll on the internet shows that online marketers who are doing affiliate marketing can earn anywhere between thousands of dollars yearly to even millions when you have set up your business properly.

Reason 4 – The Sales Performance Can Be Easily Measured

The scalability of any affiliate marketing program is another of the reasons why it is perfect for a beginner. The entire process is very transparent and you will not have too much on your plate. This is extremely helpful especially for beginners who cannot handle complex matters of business. In case you ever feel like the work is becoming too much for single-handed operation, you can always hire some additional people and yet invest much less than other businesses. This is because you are going to save a huge amount of money on office space as a business in affiliate marketing does not necessarily require you to have a physical office space. Measuring the performance of your sales is much easier in businesses dealing with affiliate marketing.

Reason 5 – You Will Have the Freedom to Sell What You Want

With affiliate marketing, you will never be pressurized or forced to sell or do anything that you do not want to. So, with professional independence, you can also choose the brands with whom you want to work with. Thus, your integrity will remain intact and you will have the opportunity to remain honest to yourself. Nobody will have the right to push products to you that you personally think are not worth it to promote. You will get to speak about only those products that you believe in or would have bought yourself. That's the beauty of affiliate marketing. Just think about it – you will be earning money by promoting products that you actually love. How cool is that!

Reason 6 – Affiliate Marketing Generates Commission Per Sale

Although the rate of commission generated differs from one affiliate marketing program to the other, but hey, look on the bright side! You are actually getting paid for every product sold. But when you end up working with companies, they can give you a fixed rate of commission. With affiliate marketing, the amount of money you make will progressively increase with the number of sales.

Reason 7 – It is Perfect For Those Who Always Love to Be Amidst Competition

With affiliate marketing, you always have to deal with tons of competitions. Your site metrics might not be the same every month. Moreover, there will be several affiliate marketing sites that pop up from time to time and some of them might even be good enough to take away your audience. So, audience retention is a huge aspect and something to be mastered if you want to do well with affiliate marketing. There are several marketing strategies that you can apply and we will talk about them later on in this book. But with each change in your strategy, you must always look out for any development in your metrics. You must also keep an eye out for any negative development. If any strategy is not working out in your favor, you need to stop implementing it. So, coming up with newer strategies to stay on top of the competition ladder is one of the things that you have to be good in. So, affiliate marketing is definitely the perfect option for those who love some eternal competition.

Reason 8 – You Might Even Get Sign-Up Bonus

Some affiliate marketing programs can even grant you an instant bonus amount for signing up with them. Are you wondering about why are they giving you a bonus? Well, it is because if you are just a beginner, there will be some time before which you earn some commission through your first sale. But the bonus is meant to give you a headstart and will also keep you motivated.

Reason 9 – No Hassles of Customer Support

With affiliate marketing, you do not actually have to deal with the customers as you are only promoting the product. But with companies, the scenario is completely different. The hassles of customer support are pretty real. When after making a purchase, a customer is unhappy with what he/she received, they can put the blame of the company and then the company has to come up with a proper grievance redressal mechanism. But you do not have to worry about customer satisfaction. Your only work is to link the seller with the consumer. All the complaints from the side of the consumer will be dealt with by the seller.

So, now that you have got a basic idea, you should know about some basic facts about affiliate marketing that would push you further towards starting it right now.

- The power of affiliate marketing is now being leveraged by 84% of publishers and 81% of brands in the United States every year. This statistic is not going to decrease any time soon but is only going to increase further.
- It has been calculated that the United States notices a 10.1% increase on a yearly basis in the spending towards affiliate marketing. So, the estimate states that if this

continues at the same rate, then the number would rise to $6.8 billion by the year 2020.

- According to the stats, the costs generated in content marketing are much lesser and amounts to about only 62% of the costs that are required for the schemes of traditional marketing. Moreover, out of all the orders that are placed online, 16% comprises those made through affiliate marketing.

- The structure of the Amazon affiliate program was changed in the month of March in 2017 after which the passive income of creators dramatically increased because the rated provided by the company were raised to the range of 1-10%.

So, if you are just starting with your online business, affiliate marketing would be the best way to go about it. There is no shortage of products and you can even create your niche. If you are someone who is passionate about sports gear or photography gear, then you can expand on that same niche and create a blog or YouTube channel around it. Or, you can also create a website whereby you will be reviewing products belonging to different categories. There is no right or wrong way to do it and that is the best thing. You do what you feel would work for you. But cultivating an audience should be your first step because, without an audience, you are nothing. You will make money only when someone takes your recommendations and makes a purchase. You can even choose to make it personal by establishing yourself and proving your credibility in your niche. With time, you will be able to establish your blog or website and you will become an expert in the eyes of your audience. It is true that affiliate marketing will not fetch you money overnight. But when you stick to it and continue doing it for a long time, you will get success.

Another term that is not consequently used with affiliate marketing is the concept of influencers. When you become an expert and gather an audience, people will follow you for making their own decisions. The hyper-focused niches of influencers are now getting more priority and thus more traffic. The audience that they send to the various websites is highly credible and also shows much higher conversion rates.

So, if you are indeed planning on diving into the world of making money online, affiliate marketing would be the one that will not require too much investment and you can start straight away. Gain control of the life you lead and the income you make and you will see how your entire life changes. Although your skills will play a very crucial role in your success as an affiliate, with a consistent and intelligent approach, meeting your income goals is not something difficult. Read this book and you will learn about all the tips and tricks you need to know to excel in this field. Get higher engagement rates and convert your audience faster with these strategies. If you are not feeling confident enough, then you can always start with affiliate marketing as your second job and then gradually, when you seem some considerable income growth, you can make it your primary source of income.

Chapter 2: How And Where To Find The Idea About Which Products To Sell?

Doing well in an affiliate marketing business is every marketer's dream but first, you need to carve a niche for yourself. This means that you need to find the right type of affiliate products to sell. Affiliate marketing definitely seems incredible but everything can go wrong if your products don't sell. Making a living completely based on affiliate marketing can be tough and this is proven by the statistics which states that 90% of the total sales and conversions are achieved by only some of the affiliates amounting to less than 10%.

So, now let's dive into the topic of how you are going to find the best niche for your business.

Step 1 – Research and Find Your Niche

For those who are not aware of what a niche is, it is basically a market or category of highly specialized items. For example, organic shampoos. Normal shampoos have a vast market but when you think about organic shampoos, the market automatically becomes smaller and so does the competition. Moreover, there is also a smaller audience who are specifically interested in organic shampoos. This way, you can target them easily and focus better on your conversion tactics.

Here is one thing that you can do to figure out your niche. Search on Google with the keyword 'Top 100 websites' and there will be several websites that list the real-time data displaying the traffic that each of these websites receive. From these lists, you can figure out which sites receive maximum audience. You do not have to emulate the content but you can find out the niche.

Some of the evergreen markets in the world of affiliate marketing that usually appear higher up in the search results are health, romance and wealth. Some of the major markets in the health niche include weight management, fitness supplements, smoking issues and so on. Products related to diabetes are also on the top ranks because diabetes is now a growing problem. The primary reason why you should get started with a health niche is that people are concerned about their health more than anything else and so there is a chance that you are going to get big spenders if you use the right strategies.

Romance niches are mostly about online dating, sexual wellness and attracting someone of the opposite sex. In today's world, people are always on the lookout for a life partner or a companion and so you will get an audience that is willing to learn more.

The wealth niche comprises of topics like employment, gambling, Forex and so on. People are always looking for information on how they can make more money and so this niche is truly evergreen.

But these major markets have sub-niches too and you should choose something that you are passionate about. To develop the smaller niches, you can go to Quora and put the broader niche as your search term. You will get to know about a variety of topics that people are really interested about.

Step 2 – Check the Monetization Options

Don't start with any niche straightaway. If you have decided on a particular niche, you must also check what monetization scope it has. Starting out with affiliate marketing will do you no good if you cannot monetize your niche. ClickBank is one of the best places to search for monetization options.

When you visit the website, there is an option 'Affiliate Marketplace' on the top panel. Click on it. You will find the search bar on the next page and you can enter the category of your products which will help you narrow down your search. But the website also has some already curated lists which are shown on the left-hand side of the screen. Select the category you want and then search for your respective niche. When the results are displayed, you might find it a bit overwhelming if you are a first time user. Each search result that you see is something that the page is suggesting you to sell.

But to make the entire thing easier, you must sort your results by 'Gravity'. The main purpose of this metric is to let you know how well a product in a certain niche sells. Once you get the search results, look at the products and then decide for yourself whether they will be easy to sell or not. The search results will even show you the average income you can make from selling those products.

Step 3 – Check With Google AdWords

Checking the cost per click of keywords is another crucial step while selecting a niche for your affiliate marketing business. If you want to make more sales, you have to drive in more traffic and traffic is directly related to the competition in a particular niche. The Keyword Planner of Google AdWords is the best place to start. You should search the keywords based on phrase or category. So, select the respective option for that and then type the keywords related to your niche. Here, you should type in related words to your niche as well so that the search results can be diverse.

Once you have entered the keywords, click on 'Get Ideas'. Here you need to check the competition, average monthly searches and suggested bids. You will come to know about the traffic that these keywords get on a monthly basis. With the competition stats, you will understand the difficulty level of these keywords and how much effort you have to put in order to rank high in them. The suggested bid column simply gives you the data to signify whether or not this keyword is worth spending your time and money on.

Click on the column of 'Suggested Bids' and your results will be automatically listed in an order having the niches that pay a high amount for a single click on top. Now, inspect the results and see if there is something that suits you and then you can go back to ClickBank and do some further research on that niche in order to come up with better results.

Step 4 – Start With Virtual Products

There are both physical and digital products in the world of affiliate marketing and you have to make a choice regarding which ones you want to sell. Virtual or digital products include things like e-books, software and music but on the other hand, physical stuff includes a variety of things like gadgets, furniture, cosmetics and so on.

If you are just starting off, virtual products would be easier to deal with. Virtual products are instantly delivered to the customer once they pay the money and so there is no hassle or delay in shipping. So, if the customer needs something on an urgent basis, for example a book, they might opt for an e-book rather than a physical book. Moreover, with virtual products, you can reach a wider audience. Shipping is not always done to all parts of the world and so that is exactly where the virtual products come of help. Also, there will never be issues like products being out of stock as there is not physical product involved. So, even if you don't have to deal with the customers directly, you do have to depend on constant sales. But at the end of the day, the decision will always be in your own hands as to which products you want to sell.

Now that you know all about how you can find the products to sell or how you can figure out your niche, it is time for you to figure out where you can get these products. Finding the best affiliate programs is also important when it comes to generating handsome commissions from sales. So, here are some of the major websites when it comes to the best affiliate programs and you can find a wide variety of products to sell from them.

Amazon

Amazon is not only the biggest website in terms of affiliate marketing program but it is also the go-to website of every person willing to purchase some item. There is not a single product that you cannot find on this website. It practically has everything. Here are some reasons which will convince you to join the affiliate marketing program of this website –

- People have their faith on Amazon and they trust the website because they that the delivery of their products is guaranteed.
- As already mentioned earlier, Amazon is known for listing everything, even the weirdest products in the world.
- The upsell capability of Amazon is outstanding and this means that you are going to get some good commission too. This is because the commission is not only valid for the product you referred them to but also on all other products they buy from Amazon.
- The rates of commission at Amazon start at 4-5% and the more sales you make, your rate will become higher and higher.

ClickBank

ClickBank has over 500,000 members across the world and it also has an endless list of products that you can promote. This site is one of the major sources of all types of digital products. You should use ClickBank because –

- The pool of products on this website is quite huge.

- They will also provide you with real-time review reports which will help you to analyze your performance by monitoring, sales, refunds and cancellations data.

Rakuten

This website was previously known by the name of LinkShare. Its affiliate marketing service is quite well-established. The main characteristic of this website is that they generally work with those companies who operate on a large-scale basis and have aspects like annual sales and marketing budget. Rakuten is popular among affiliate marketers because of the following reasons –

- You will get an updated report on your performance as an affiliate.
- Both long-term and short-term marketing goals can be catered with the help of this website.
- Their affiliate marketing service is easier to work with form affiliates because they operate on an enterprise level.

ShareASale

From business services to organic products, ShareASale has everything that you need. But you must know that they will charge you a small sum as their signup fees. They also charge a small amount of money for every sale you make. This is mainly because their range of products is vast and they already have a strong market. But some of the reasons why people choose ShareASale are as follows –

- Different types of ads are supported by the website like pop-ups, image ads and so on.
- They keep a track on your progress and they also send reports from time to time. You can access your progress statistics anytime you want.
- They even provide different types of documentation and training videos to its affiliates as a part of the membership.
- If you are stuck in a problem, the website has a dedicated support team to help you navigate through anything you want.
- They work with a wide array of merchants and publishers belonging to different sectors.

eBay

Being one of the oldest stores online, eBay is still highly popular today. With over 5 million sellers and 162 million shoppers, the website has millions of products that you will find relevant to your niche. Another great thing about eBay is that it is open worldwide to about 13 countries at present. So, if you are planning to tap into global customers, eBay can be the door to success. Here are some more reasons why you should consider joining the affiliate program of eBay –

- You can access the database and so personalization of your feed is possible and easy.
- eBay gives you the opportunity to come up with links for every single listing and so you can share them on your social media.
- Their customer services are available in five different languages in the different countries.
- All the latest tips and trends that circulate in the world of affiliate marketing will be sent to you by eBay.
- Their reports and analytics are quite user-friendly and easy to decipher even for a layman.

So, if you want to start your journey as an affiliate, these websites can serve as your starting point and then you can continue spreading your reach.

Chapter 3: How To Create The Right Type Of Website To Drive Traffic?

Not everyone has an idea of what they are doing when they create their first affiliate marketing website. As an affiliate marketer, a large chunk of your time will go into creating promotional content, building strong and long-term relationships with brands and also pushing yourself to walk the extra mile in order to make your content stand out from others. Creating a website that can drive in profitable sales is not all about SEO. There are a lot of factors that you must take into consideration.

The golden rule of being a successful affiliate marketer is to know the tricks of marketing yourself well. If you want to become a full-time marketer, you will have to attract thousands of visitors to your site and for that, you need to be fully aware of the hacks of promoting yourself to the world. This does not happen overnight and takes a lot of dedication.

You can start your website on WordPress because it is not only cheap but also way easier to handle. If you are not yet familiar with how WordPress works, don't worry because this guide will teach you everything that you need to know in order to set up your website. The services of WordPress are completely free but there are two important things that you need to purchase and those are – domain name and web hosting.

Domain Name – The URL people enter for reaching your website is the domain name. To get your website's own unique domain name, you will have to get the registration done with a domain registrar. Now, the terms might seem intimidating but the process is not.

Web Hosting – A web host serves the role of making your website visible to the rest of the world. In simpler words, you are basically paying rent to a web server.

These two are the most important things that you need to take care of for building a successful affiliate marketing website. Now, there are several places where you can avail these services for free but if you are serious about affiliate marketing, it is always advised not to approach the free services. This is because in some cases, the site that you approach for these services might even hold a certain portion of the right to your content. That doesn't sound good, does it? Thus, to put it in a simpler manner, the business that you are spending time to build might not even be yours completely. Alternatively, when you get your own website, you will have control over everything.

So, if you are not sure where to start, here is a step by step breakdown of the entire process to make it easier.

Step 1 – Choose a Good Domain Name

Choosing your domain name should be done with considerable thought because it has to be something authoritative. Your domain name, if not chosen correctly, can even limit your website's potential in the future. For example, if you choose something like topaudiogadgets.com then your niche automatically gets narrowed down to audio gadgets and you wouldn't want that for your website. If in another couple of months, you want to review an air conditioner, you wouldn't be able to do so just because your website name says audio gadgets. But something like thetechadvisor.com can open a lot of doors for you as you can review any tech-related products. Long-term thinking should be your first priority if you want to make your business a success in the future.

Here are some tips to keep in mind while you are choosing the domain name for your website.

- **It should be easy to type** – The more the number of words in the domain, the more difficult it will be for your audience to remember it. So, you should keep it short and simple and yet catchy so that they can remember it after just a single glance. Multiple spellings are another problem that can meddle up the brains of your audience. For example, some people may write the word 'express' in their domain name as 'xpress'. Now, this may seem cool in the first instant but it won't be so cool when your audience is unable to remember the correct spelling and hence, ends up landing at some other website.

- **The name should have appropriate keywords** – There are several ways in which you can churn out ideas for names that will fit your website. For starters, why not come up with something that is directly related to your business or the category of products you write about? Or, you can also simply base your website on your own name. But the presence of a strong keyword would definitely play a big role. The implementation of keywords in a domain name is very smart. There are tons of SEO benefits to it. Ranking your website higher in the results of search engines is the ultimate goal and putting keywords in the domain name will only help that dream come true faster. Also, when you use the potential keywords in your domain name, any visitor to your site will instantly get to know what your niche is and what your website is about.

- **You can use a domain generator** – In case you are out of ideas, you can always leave the task of brainstorming to a domain generator. But you can only take those names which have not already been taken. For example, you cannot name your blog thewirecutter.com because the name has already been taken.

- **Avoid the usage of hyphens and numbers** – While you are coming up with ideas, avoid using hyphens and numbers at all because they often create misunderstandings. For example, if you say your website name is top10products.com, someone listening to you might think it is toptenproducts.com and then they would not be able to find your website.

- **The domain name extension has to be chosen carefully** – The extensions at the end of your domain name also have a role to play (.com, .net, and so on). The most popular one out of all the extensions is the .com one but getting a short and catchy name in a .com extension can be tricky as it is usually already taken. Here are some of the other extensions that are usually used but they also have their own meanings – .me (for personal sites and blogs), .org (for nonprofits and organizations that are non-commercial in nature), .net(for websites related to tech-based subjects), .info (for websites that are mainly informational) and .co (that is generally used as an abbreviation for a variety of words like community, commerce and, more popularly, company).

Step 2 – Buy Your Domain Name

Once you have finalized the name of your domain and made sure that it is available, it is time for you to finally make the purchase. There are a wide range of options for you to choose from when it comes to companies from whom you can buy the domain. Some of the major accredited domain registrars are HostGator, GoDaddy, A2 Hosting, Bluehost, Pantheon and so on.

Choose any website you want and then enter the domain name that you have selected in their search panel. You will automatically be show whether that name is available or not. If it is available, then you have to proceed with it and make the necessary payment after which the domain will be yours. But you will also have to enter some details as you are literally getting the domain registered to your name. Once you have bought the domain, the next step is to get web hosting.

Step 3 – Choose a Good Web Hosting Company

Creating quality content may not yield fruitful results if your web hosting is not right and so you need to take web hosting seriously. Your web hosting will determine how responsive your site is. James Lyne, who is a Forbes contributor, had stated that every day, over 30,000 websites are hacked. And do you know the reason behind this? They all made wrong choices when it came to web hosting. Of course, there is no perfect solution to this problem but you can always be a bit more careful in order to prevent such mishaps from happening with you. Whenever you choose a web hosting company, you can stay assured about the fact that they update their database from time to time so that they are ready to deal with any potential threats.

But if you want to make the right decision while choosing your web hosting company, here are some essential tips for you.

- **Decide on the type of web host that would suit you best** – Your web hosting options can easily be narrowed down if you start analyzing and understanding the specific needs of your business. For example, if you are going to open a review website with all the affiliate marketing links that also has high-quality videos, then your hosting will definitely need to be with someone who can provide high responsiveness. Moreover, if you are going to open a website that is going to receive a high amount of traffic, then you cannot do so on a shared server. Shared servers are suitable only for websites that have a fixed list of demands.

- **Choosing the appropriate hosting package is important** – Many beginners start with shared hosting packages because they are much cheaper and thus affordable for someone who doesn't want to invest much. But they also have greater risks. The biggest problem that these shared hosting packages have is that they will provide you with a way slower website response time. This can drive off your audience who do not have the patience to wait eternally for your website to load. On the other hand, VPS or Virtual Private Servers can provide much better performance.

- **Read the reviews before settling for a company** – Just like any other product, settling for a web hosting company before reading any of the reviews would be a big mistake. Reviews denote how reliable these websites are. While reading reviews, you might even uncover complaints from past or present users and you can even check whether or not the company puts any effort to solve these problems.

- **Choose the right bandwidth** – When your website is new, it is obvious that it won't require too much bandwidth. But you must always go for a bandwidth amount that leaves space for future growth. Moreover, you should also check whether the web hosting company provides flexible options regarding upgrading your hosting plan later on. This way, you can always go to the higher rung on the ladder when your business demands you to.

- **Don't get tempted by a lower price** – When you are just starting off, it is easier to fall to the temptation created by certain companies by offering hosting services at a cheaper rate. But you should not fall for that trap.

Don't ever get fixated on the price. Always remember that these companies are not doing anything for free. They are charging less and so they will also give poorer service. It can be anything like a slower server, constant downtime, unresponsive customer support and so on.

- **Don't skim through the Terms of Service** – Always remember that this is your own business and so don't just sign up with something where you don't even know the terms. Think of it as an investment of time towards reaping the benefits in the future. It is true that everyone skips through the part where you have to accept the Terms and Conditions but don't do that, at least not with this. Moreover, you should also keep an eye out for any type of refund policy which these web hosting service providers sometimes have.

- **See whether they have a backup plan** – You should always be assured of a Plan B in case everything goes south. Ask your web hosting company what measures they take in case all your data on the site is lost. In case they give an answer with which you are not satisfied, don't avail their services. It is always better to be safe than sorry.

- **Enquire about security features** – Security breaches can happen at any time and to anyone and so to stay on the safe side, you need to be sure that your web hosting company has taken all the necessary precautionary measures. Enquire about their security features and how do they intend to protect the private information of their customers.

- **Avoid new companies** – There is nothing wrong with new companies but you will have to think about your own good. New companies who have just entered the market might provide you with amazing deals on their packages but they do not have the experience to handle growth. So, if you rely on them for web hosting, it might happen that your site will suffer later on. Thus, it is always advisable to get web hosting from an experienced company.

- **See whether they provide extra features** – In case you need extra features like an SSL certificate or email hosting, then you need to check with the web hosting company beforehand.

No matter what company you are choosing, make sure your hosting plan supports WordPress. This is because it is the easiest website builder and as a beginner, it is the platform you should use to build your website.

Step 4 – Create Your Essential Website Pages

In your arsenal of affiliate marketing, your website is the strongest tool you have. So, it needs to be comprehensive and all-encompassing. Once you have completed your website hosting, it is time for you to start creating your website. Now there are some pages which form the skeleton of an affiliate marketing website and your first task would be to construct them. They are as follows –

- **About page** – This page should have a personal touch. This is the page that would give your visitors an idea about who you are and why you are doing this. But the popular belief states that the About page is entirely about the author or owner of the website. This is not at all true. The About page should also focus on how you can be helpful to your readers and how your content is unique and reliable. The goal of an About page is not about telling your life story when it comes to affiliate marketing. Rather, it is more about converting your audience.

- **Home page** – This is the page that will open to your audience the moment they come to your website. So, the importance of this website is completely transparent. It should be engrossing. You can choose a variety of themes on WordPress in order to come up with an attractive design for your Home page. You can even make it an amalgamation of some of the latest reviews you have on your website.

- **Contact page** – This page is crucial too as this is how various brands will reach out to you for collaboration. This is also the page your readers will use in case they have something to ask about. This page can get you some seriously potential leads and so no mistake should be tolerated while constructing this page. Moreover, it should be easy to navigate. You should also keep your social media links on this page in case your audience wants to follow you there. Moreover, the link to your Contact page should be prominently placed in the Navigation Menu of your website so that the visitors do not face any difficulty in finding it.

Step 5 – Write Your First Post

Once you are done with constructing the basic pages, it is time for you to write your first post. Regardless of the niche that you have chosen, there are certain types of posts that are popular in the world of affiliate marketing. You can start with any of them.

- **'How to' guides** – These are one of the most popular blog posts. You, as an affiliate, can construct an informative blog post showing your readers how they can use a certain product or how they can do something within a budget. It can be something like 'How to build a smart home under $100'. You can either write an article like this which will combine a variety of products or base your articles on a single product and give a complete guide on it. But make sure that the chunks of information you include are easy to understand and have proper readability. You should also anticipate the questions that your audience might have and answer them in your guides.

- **Simple product reviews** – If you want to start off with something less complicated, then product reviews are exactly what you should choose. The rating system you use should be understandable and simple. The content must be well-researched and every aspect of the product should be discussed. Make the review honest because only then will your audience develop faith in your opinion. Most importantly, don't back off from giving negative opinions because they are equally important.

- **Product comparisons** – These are another type of popular articles as they address the dilemma that everyone faces while purchasing an item. The focus of your article should be placed on providing every single detail about a product that a viewer could ask for. Your writing style should be more educational and less promotional. It should add value to a customer who is trying to choose between two competing products.

- **Best of lists** – These are basically articles that deal with a particular category like the 'Best Lipsticks of 2019'. These should inform the audience about products that are currently at the top of their category and what specialties do they have which makes them unique.

You can also consider making you first a video rather than a written article. Videos grab more attention mostly because people enjoy watching something rather than reading about it.

Moreover, it will also have the potential to reach a wide range of audience.

So, these were the steps that you should follow in order to construct a website that can bring in a lot of traffic every month and thus generate sales.

Chapter 4: How To Leverage Social Media Sites?

Leveraging your social media sites will give you a high amount of traffic if done in the right manner. According to the statistics given by Nielson, users of the internet that spend their time on social media amount to 23% and among those users, 70% engage in online shopping. So, these statistics alone are enough to prove the importance of capitalization of your social media platforms.

So, here are some ways in which you can make the best use of the social media sites at your disposal –

Step 1 – Choose the Right Social Media Platform

Careful consideration has to be done while you are making your choice regarding which social media platform you want to use for your affiliate marketing business. The choice you make is important because of the following reasons –

- When you choose the right platform, you will have access to the right audience who will be genuinely interested in the products you promote. Thus, driving in more traffic would not seem much difficult. Moreover, social media will also help you to expand through likes, shares, and follows.
- Making the right decision will allow you to make the best use of your resources. Thus, improved sales and increased web traffic are guaranteed.

But, if you want to make the right decision with respect to your social media platform here are some tips that you should follow –

Refine your goals with audience demographics – You will have website visitors from a varied number of sources. The audience demographics are the metrics that will help you to categorize your audience. The basis of categorization includes a variety of factors like gender, income, age, location and so on.

Now you must be thinking how audience demographics can help you choose the right social media platform. Well, the answer is simple. With these stats, you will know where exactly does your audience socialize and secondly, what is the type of content they prefer the most.

There are two different ways in which you can use the demographics of your audience.

- *Use Google Analytics.* The data acquisition part is the most important step. You not only have to track where your audience is from but you also have to study their behavior on your site. For example, if you notice that most of your visitors like to share your content on a certain social media platform then you can use that information to your advantage. This will also help you narrow down your options when it comes to social media.

- *Use this data and compare it with the social media platforms.* Once you have acquired the data from Google Analytics, your next step would be to approach the known social media platforms and then compare your data with their demographics. General demographics like gender, location and age can also be used. In this way, you will find the social media platform which best matches the type of audience you have.

No matter what strategy you use, statistically-obtained data is always the best when it comes to studying your audience and increasing the returns on your campaigns.

Your choice should be in line with your business goals – Whatever choice you make regarding your social media, it should completely be in line with the goals you have in business. But if you are not sure how to do that then here are three basic steps that you should follow –

- *There has to be a main goal.* This is the goal that determines what result you want out of your social media campaign, whether it is expanding your reach or building your traffic. So, from there you can move forward with the rest of the process.
- *Build an action plan.* Once you have selected your ultimate goal, your next step would be to frame the path you want to follow. For example, if traffic building is what you are aiming at, then coming up with a lot of clickable content should be on top of your list. But if you want to expand your reach, then coming up with content that is shareable is what you should do.
- *Find the medium for your actions.* If you are preparing shareable content, then the two best mediums are Facebook and Pinterest. But if you want to drive in more traffic to your site, then you should aim at Twitter while on the other hand, Instagram can come in quite handy when it comes to expanding your reach.

Know the limits of your resources – Of course, unlimited resources are something what every business owner could have profited from but sadly, that is something not present with everyone. So, you have to do an honest assessment of the time, commitment and money limitations that you might face. Your platform selection should be done only after you have done a full assessment of all the limitations you have. Here is a two-step process that you can follow to make things easier –

- *Uncover all the possible limits you have in all aspects.* Every social media campaign requires some amount of time and effort from your part. So, it is your job to determine beforehand how much of those factors can you truly devote to your campaign.

- *Choose the platform that aligns with your limitations.* This will become clearer with an example. So, if you want to churn out the best possible results out of your social media, then Facebook can be handled with around 1-2 posts on a daily basis, Twitter's best performance can be achieved with 10-15 posts and 5-10 on Pinterest will work perfectly fine. But one of the most important things that you should keep in mind is your budget. This will ensure that you make the right decision and receive a decent amount of ROI or Return on Investment.

What you must understand that even if your resources are limited, it does not necessarily mean that you will have a poor social media campaign. You just have to play it smart.

Step 2 – Build a High-Quality Following

Creating your account on the right platform of social media is just the beginning of a long journey. The next steps are when all the hard work begins. And you should know that there is not shortcut to this. You cannot acquire thousands of followers overnight. You have to interact with the people following you and build your credibility so that they can put their faith in you. According to statistics, it has been noticed that 17 per cent users of the internet feel more reassured about a brand when they see their online presence. So, here are a few tips that you can keep in mind if you want to build a quality following –

- *Follow people in your network.* One of the first steps of growing your following is to follow other people on the social media platforms who are somehow related to your niche. Surround yourself with positive vibes and people who are likeminded. This way you will also stay updated on the different hacks others are using in their affiliate marketing business.
- *Keep up with the consistency of posts.* You should post your content once in a while. You have to be consistent if you want some real results. The best way to maintain this is to make a schedule. This will keep all of your posts organized and you don't have to be worried. Moreover, concentrate on one platform at a time. If you keep juggling between the various social media platforms, you will not be able to see any positive results. Make a

content calendar and everything will start falling into place. The key to maximizing the engagement on your posts is to time your posts so that you do not have to do that in real-time. Also, don't repeat your content. Make it unique and it will receive all the love they deserve.

- *Provide some real value through your information.* Your posts must be informational. If you are reviewing a certain product as an affiliate, your post must be detailed and unbiased. Only then will your audience rely on your before taking any final purchase decision. If your audience finds your posts relatable, they you can assume the role of an authoritative person in that niche. Your posts should concern the real-life problems or any questions that your audience might have when they buy the same product. This will, in turn, increase the number of shares and retweets of your posts.

- *Don't forget entertainment value.* Humor can popularize your content in a great way. Moreover, it plays a crucial role in humanizing your brand. People are attracted to light-hearted discussions rather than something which is grim and serious. Your content should discuss serious matters but in a friendly and smooth manner,

- *Be responsive.* Always stay on alert once you have made a post on social media. Your audience needs you to be present for every query they have. Respond to the comments they leave. If your audience has some additional question on the product or service that you have just reviewed, don't back off from answering those questions. Working that extra bit shows that you really care for your audience and that they can turn to you for any help they want.

- *Your focus should be on helping and not selling*. Sales are obviously important otherwise you will not be making any revenue. But concentrating solely on the selling part will not earn you any real following or audience on social media. If there is some specific problem that has been buzzing your followers, take the leap and make some content surrounding it. That content will spread like wildfire because it is something that you audience has been craving for.

- *Be social and don't just concentrate on numbers*. Your social media following is just a number but your aim should be building a solid relationship with your audience. It is always better to have a handful of 1000 followers who are highly active and engaging rather than 100,000 followers who do not care about you at all. Realize the beauty of social media which gives you the power of making friends from all around the world. Don't be arrogant. Be open-minded and embrace everyone with a big heart.

- *Post video content too*. Video content is now spreading faster. Moreover, Live videos can bring you way better engagement than normal posts. So, don't simply stick to text-based posts and expand your horizons.

Step 3 – Build an Effective Posting Strategy

Now that you have discovered the platforms that work best for your business and the ways in which you can build a following, it is time for you to construct a posting strategy. Successive ads are not the way to go about it. Remember that social media is your virtual family. So, imagine if someone in your party keeps blabbering about how they are so cool and how their work is so amazing, do you feel attracted to that person? No, right? Instead, what happens is that you feel least interested and tag that person as an obsessed and self-centered human. The same things holds true for your different social media platforms.

Your posts should have a diversity in them. There is rule of posting that is followed widely and is known as the 4-1-1 rule. Read on to find more about it.

The 4-1-1 rule stands for –

- 4 – sharing four relevant, new and unique posts from others in the world of internet who are quite established influencers themselves
- 1 – re-sharing one content from someone who belongs to the pool of audience you have
- 1 – one post that is action-oriented and self-promotional

The rule should be followed diligently and you should not mess with it in any way if you want good results. Arrange your promotional calendar accordingly and keep one-month worth of content ready beforehand so that you do not have to stress about anything at the last moment. Most importantly, don't make the mistake of repeating content! This is extremely important otherwise your audience will lose interest in you and turn to someone else who can give them more unique and updated info.

Now if you are wondering how does the 4-1-1 rule work, well then read along and you'll find out.

- Firstly, the rule demands you to share content from other influencers who have already built their credibility. When you share their content, people will form a perception about you as a thought leader. Consequently, you will start gaining credibility too. In the eyes of your readers, you start gaining that authority which the influencers (whose content you are sharing) already have. But what you must be careful about is choosing the content which you share. The content should align with the type of content that you produce as well.

- Secondly, the rule involves re-sharing your audience's content. Now, this step will help you form a strong bond with those present in your audience and deepen your engagement. When you share their content, they will become more encouraged to share your content in return as well.

- Now, once you have completed both of the above-mentioned steps, you can release one self-promotional content. By this point, your audience will take the self-promotion well because you have already established your base. Now when you post this self-promotional content, it should be addressing your audience's concerns and not solely be based on you or what you think about it. Your views are obviously important but you must also think about the several questions that could crop up in the minds of your audience and answer all those questions beforehand. This way, your audience will find your posts comprehensive.

- You should also give some call-to-action posts from time to time. These posts should develop a sense of scarcity in the minds of your audience. For example, you can release a promo code for your audience or you can give a discount on a certain product after collaborating with a brand. But make sure these discounts and codes last only for a certain amount of time so that the audience is pumped up to take action now! You can also build reciprocity in your audience by promising them a small gift along with the purchase they make with your affiliate link. You can also ask them to write a testimonial for your affiliate website so that it can produce a social proof of your credibility to others. You can then, in turn, post those testimonials on your website and social media and gather newer audience.

Don't get disheartened if you don't see any fruitful results at first. It is totally natural as achieving success on social media is a step-by-step process and takes time. Implement the tracking parameters and keep a regular analysis of your growth because this will help you understand which strategies are working best for your case. If you maintain a disciplined and regular approach, building a strong foothold and creating your own tribe online is possible. The greater your following and reach, the more commissions you will earn.

Chapter 5: How To Use Paid Advertising To Make Money Faster?

One of the very initial dilemmas that almost every affiliate marketer has to face is that whether they should move forward with paid traffic or just stick to free traffic. Well, free traffic might definitely seem alluring because of the simple fact that they are free but in the long run, free traffic would not help you to reach a wider audience especially with all the new algorithm trends coming into the market. There are tons of content creators all over the world and everyone is trying in some way or the other to sell their content. So, if you stick to free traffic, it will be years before you witness any real growth.

Free traffic would require you to have outstanding SEO skills and that is something you will be able to utilize in your business. But a little bit of paid advertising never hurts.

So, before we get into the details of how you can use paid advertising, you need to know the benefits of the process so that you can get motivated into using it for your affiliate marketing business.

Thus, here are few of the benefits that you can enjoy from paid advertising –

- **Faster growth** – As already mentioned above, free traffic is good but if you want to climb the ladder of growth faster, paid advertising can really benefit you from that sense. If you are still skeptical then analyze the competition present and you should do this comparison with the other long-standing websites in the same niche. Check who has a stronger domain authority as compared to you and the process of narrowing down will become easier. Getting constant free traffic is a cumbersome procedure especially because of all the factors that play a role in it. And so, if you learn the tricks of paid advertising, you can establish your base faster.

  Why wait for years when you can start making something fruitful out of your affiliate marketing effort right from today? Once you start optimizing, growth will become prominent instantly and PPC advertising or pay-per-click advertising is the best method to target the right audience. See your posts rank higher than before once you implement the right strategies of paid advertising.

- **More targeted reach** – When you use only SEO techniques in your growth process, you may not always be reaching the right audience, or let's just say, the right target audience. Thus, you might not be attracting the right type of visitors who might actually buy something. Take this for an example. You have a blog post on a certain brand of sports shoes that you have affiliate links to. Now, once you publish that post, you will be getting views and traffic from different sources and organic Google search as well. Does this sound amazing? Well it is until one day you realize that all this traffic is not doing you any good as these people are not really buying any stuff. But the main aim of affiliate marketing is to make your audience click on your affiliate link to buy the product or service. So, what went wrong? It is simple – the target audience. When the traffic was organic, it was also disorganized and not specific. But to actually make it work, your target audience is, suppose, men belonging to the age group of 20 to 30 interested in running. So, that is something highly specific and paid advertising can help you reach that kind of audience. This will not only generate traffic but also turn them into loyal readers of your blog if your posts are captivating enough. And the best part is that all of this can be achieved within a very short time span if you use paid advertising.

- **Convert your traffic into sales** – Writing a blog post doesn't really take that much amount of time as compared to the time that you have to spend towards the design and promotion of that post. Now, as you must have heard already – time is money so don't waste it in something which is not going to be fruitful. Then, what is the solution? Well, for starters, you can divulge in paid advertising. This is because, all that experimentation and testing that you do in order to make your affiliate marketing business work is a lot time consuming, so why not make the best of the time you spend? If you depend on SEO alone, it will be years before you finally realize a sizeable income. You will spend all those months on the grind just to make yourself visible to the eyes of the world especially with this much amount of competition all around to deal with.

  On the other hand, when you use paid advertising, you are showing your content to those targeted people who might actually be interested in buying the product. Thus, in simpler terms, paid advertising will increase your conversion percentage which is directly equivalent to more sales.

- **You don't actually need a lot of investment** – One of the greatest myths of paid advertising is that it costs a lot. You know what, it doesn't! All you need is a few dollars to initially get started with the paid advertising that is present on the different social media channels. With that small amount of money, you can start targeting a specific group of audience and see if that works out for you. With a few such hit and trial experiments with advertising, you will come to know which type of audience is actually worth putting your money in because they are going to fetch you some good return. When you are just starting out, try split testing. This means, you need to divide your marketing budget into different ad campaigns and at the end of a specific time period, say 15 days, analyze which of those campaigns is performing the best. This will make the entire process of converting your audience into potential leads much easier. Just to give you an idea, an amount of $10 is enough for a solo entrepreneur to invest in his/her ad campaign per week and that will bring them quite good returns.

Now that you know about the several benefits that paid advertising can fetch you, it is time to know how you are going to do it. For starters, here are some practices that you should know about as they form the basics of paid advertising when it comes to content creation for affiliate marketing.

Tip 1 – Target the right audience

This point has been reiterated time and again in various chapters and for good reason because your audience is everything. Affiliate marketing is solely based on traffic and conversion rates. So, the first step of paid advertising will be finding out the right audience for your business. It is true that ad targeting doesn't involve a lot of steps and thus, people tend to rush along the process to save time. But this is not the place to think about how much time you are putting into it as this will literally determine the success of your business. You should devote as much time you need to pin-point exactly the audience that would be interested in buying the product you are promoting.

You might be having a great advertisement but still not making enough revenue. This is usually the case with those who do not spend the time that is required in the targeting phase. Yes, you might even have to spend hours in experimenting the different target audiences and whether they bring you returns or not. But if you think that something is off, don't step back from making adjustments and tweaks in your targeting audience because that is exactly what you need to do until and unless there is a right fit.

But if you are too afraid to take up all of this by yourself or maybe you do not have the time to do all the research required for marketing, you can set aside some budget for hiring an expert consultant on this matter. This way, you can even figure out the more profitable targeting faster.

Tip 2 – Perform a complete keyword analysis

The keywords you choose for your ads play a huge role in forming the bigger picture. They are ones that take your content to the audience and if keywords are wrong themselves, your content will be reaching the wrong people. This aspect becomes even more important when you are dealing with a platform like Google AdWords.

So, how will you find the right keywords for your content? Firstly, brainstorm all those words that your audience might use in your niche to search some relevant content. Put yourself in the shoes of a buyer and think about what you would have used as a keyword to search for the content you are looking for. These keywords are more popularly known as the 'niche keywords', the reason being their direct relation to your niche. You also have to make sure that the keywords used are in line with the intent of your content theme.

The auto-complete search bar of Google is another amazing way of looking up relevant keywords to use in your campaigns. In this way, you can get different variations of the same thing. Moreover, you will get the keywords in the order of the ones that are more commonly searched for. Keep testing different keywords and keep tweaking them which brings us to the last tip of this topic...

Tip 3 – Keep testing and adjust accordingly

This point is so important that this definitely deserves a separate mention. So, don't stop experimentation until you get the results you were craving for because if you are not getting them, the problem lies in your strategies and not anything else. Optimization and constant improvement are the secrets behind a successful ad campaign and you should never forget that.

Well, apart from these tips, you should not stress about getting it all right at the first try because it is not going to be that way. There will be downfalls too but the key is to not stop trying.

But wait, you also have to decide the platform on which you want to run these ads. The platform should be the right one for the product(s) you are writing about and it should have the target audience you need. Testing and all is fine but in order to make sure that you take an informed decision, we have curated a list of the best paid traffic sources that are usually used by affiliate marketers and how they can be good for you.

1. Google AdWords

This is nothing but the paid advertising platform of Google. Whenever you perform a search on Google, you are bound to get a couple of ads on top. Those are the advertised posts which appear at the top of the search results even before the organically listed webpages are ranked. Buy who is this type of advertising for? Well, you must know that out of all the online searches, 77% of it is occupied by Google. Thus, almost any content creator or entrepreneur can use and implement Google AdWords in their business. Such is the versatility of this amazing platform. Think about it this way – what do you do when you want to buy something? You search it on Google, right? Well, that is exactly something your readers are doing as well. People have their faith on Google for showing them the right results and thus, this also makes Google one of the best platforms for ad targeting as people will come to Google to get their queries about purchase decisions and certain products answered. And you need to keep your blog posts ready to answer all those questions.

2. Facebook Ads

Among all other social media platforms, Facebook currently stands to be the most famous one. Well, they also have the largest ads platform on social media. The different parameters used by Facebook for enhancing their ads targeting capabilities are amazing. Moreover, they keep updating their features from time to time to give you a better ad experience. The current number of active users on Facebook is 2.2 billion. Unbelievable but true. So, you will definitely be getting your target audience on Facebook. All you have to do is make the best use of all the advanced options that Facebook gives at your disposal and construct an ad campaign that yields you the right results. Another amazing feature that you can enjoy from Facebook ads is retargeting. The Facebook Pixel is a feature that can be put on your website and so this will help you attract those people's attention who have visited your website in the past. The idea behind this is that the effort required to convert a repeating visitor is much less than a new visitor.

3. **Instagram Ads**

Now that Instagram is owned by Facebook itself, the platform has undergone several major changes over the course of last few years, namely the Instagram Live and Instagram Stories. The main idea behind Instagram is to make it a platform for all the visually-appealing things. And the best part is that today there are over 600 million active users on this photo-sharing app where you can now share videos too especially with the help of IGTV, which has created a different world altogether. You can set your goals for advertisement according to your requirement. You can either run the ads to garner engagement or you can also do it with the aim of paid traffic. So, when should you actually use Instagram more than Facebook? The answer is not simple. But if the products on your affiliate marketing blog is about something that is visually appealing and the target audience is mostly young people, then Instagram can be the perfect platform to experiment your ad campaigns as a beginner.

But no matter which traffic source you choose, you should always their restrictions and regulations because they all have some. Not looking out for those restrictions and advertising just about anything would lead to warnings and permanent closure of your ad account and you definitely wouldn't want that. These restrictions usually circle around misleading banners which are constructed to attract visitors but don't really provide realistic promises. Moreover, you will not be able to promote all types of content on any mainstream ad network, for example, any adult or sensitive content.

You should also ensure proper quality of traffic. The biggest drawback plaguing every form of social media is the huge amount of bots. This is also termed as fraudulent traffic. But you must not fall into the clutches of such a sham and remind yourself that your business reputation is what matters the most. So, be careful of such activities and play with credible traffic only. Do plenty of research about everything that has been discussed in this chapter and don't leave any of the stones unturned. If you follow all these steps, success is not far away.

Chapter 6: Low Ticket Programs And High Ticket Programs

Now we come to the chapter that you were probably waiting for. Here we learn all about the low ticket and high ticket programs. The definition of a high ticket item is something that will give you a huge amount of time which you can probably use to sustain yourself for a week and in some cases, a month or even a year (yes!). This is the 'big fish' that every affiliate marketer wants to catch. Alternatively, the low ticket items mostly include things which will fetch you a small commission, for example, e-books.

Now to fully understand how these different programs can affect your sales, let's study an example. Let us say that you are currently making a revenue of $15 by selling one copy of a certain e-book. That might appear all exciting when the first sale comes in but is it enough for you to sustain yourself? No. So, in order to make, suppose $30,000 in a year, you will have to sell at least 2,000 copies of that same e-book. Now, that is something quite challenging to do.

The only way in which you can attempt to do this is by creating a website. Once you do that, you will have to devise strategies in order to direct more and more traffic to your affiliate links and maybe after a year, your website will finally be attracting 1,000 unique visitors each day. For the adverts that you place on your site, the clickthrough rate might be anywhere around 1-10% at an average and your conversion rate will also be something of the same value. This means, that in every 1-100 days, you will be making 1 sale. And you will be getting this by working day and night. So, if you now see the bigger picture, low ticket programs can surely give you sustainable revenues but only when your website has tons of different products, a huge zeal for excelling and invoking the marketing ninja inside of you and a great plan.

But on the other hand, if you sell high-ticket products that can fetch you $1,000 on per sale, then a total of 30 such products will be enough to give you $30,000 a year. And most importantly, you have 12 months to sell 30 products which definitely makes the picture a lot easier. You will not only have a sustainable income but also an extra amount of time in your hands that you can utilize in your own ways. So, do you see the world of difference between high-ticket and low-ticket programs? Having 30 happy customers is way lot easier than making each and every one of those 2000 customers happy.

There is another factor that comes into play in these low-ticket and high-ticket products. The customers buying low-ticket products are usually the ones that keep complaining about them and keep asking discounts. But the ones who are spending on the high-ticket products are easier to maintain. They are the ones that are serious enough to pay a huge amount of money on a product because they understand the value.

To steer clear of merchants that won't pay you enough commission, you should know about the features to look for in an affiliate marketing program before becoming a part of it. So, here are some of them.

High rates of conversion

The merchants perform that the best have a much higher ability to convert the traffic that they receive into potential sales. There is a term that is used in the world of affiliate marketing and it is called EPC or Earnings per Click. This term is used to denote the money that per click in an affiliate marketing program generates. But on the other hand, this term can also be used to signify the amount of money earned by the affiliate on the basis of per click. You must have understood by now how important the role of EPC is because without it, you literally cannot pinpoint the performance of the merchant. Judging merchant performance is so important because of the fact that there are so many merchants on the web that claim a lot but do not actually have any proof to show that.

But on most affiliate networks, you will be able to view the EPC data and this will assist you in making a comparison between all the closely related merchants on the web. When you see that a merchant is having a relatively low EPC value, then either that merchant is new or their conversion rates are not that good.

Fixed commission that is generous or a percentage-based system

You will come across several advertisers who pay very low commission rates – either in the low double-digits or sometimes even in single digits. Just steer clear of such people as they are not worth your time. Any advertiser who is willing to pay you a sustainable rate of commission will definitely have the aim of building a relationship that is mutually beneficial and profitable. Hence, they usually know how they should be appreciative about the work put forward by the affiliates.

A low threshold for payout

Whenever the payout threshold is low, you will automatically have more enthusiasm and motivation to work towards that affiliate marketing program for the simple reason that you will get to access your payment faster. There are merchants that have no threshold value for payouts while some have the minimum value set to $100. But when most affiliate networks are considered, the standard threshold value for payout is $50. But anything above $100 is unjust.

A cookie length of minimum one month

When marketers are allowed only a few days to make their traffic convert, it is not fair because that timeframe is too low for anyone. For the prospects to finally become consumers, the marketers should be allowed a month so that they can reap the benefits of their promotional effort. The standard industry practice is giving a 30-day referral period but what should be made commonplace is a span of 90 days.

Deep linking capabilities

The capability possessed by an affiliate to create a link directing to a very specific webpage on the site of the merchant is called deep linking. An example will make this clear. Suppose, the affiliate can give a link to an article that will somehow connect to his post in place of giving any old-school generic affiliate link directing to a homepage. This entire system gives greater success when it comes to conversion of traffic for the sole reason that the potential audience is being sent to landing pages that already possess targeted content. The affiliate tracking apps that are available in the market often offer deep linking options but in some cases the option has to be enabled by the advertisers.

A high-performing affiliate tracking software

Every idea's success has a cornerstone and when it comes to affiliate marketing, the tracking software becomes a cornerstone. The software should not only have dashboards that are user-friendly but also a tracking system that is smooth and reliable. All of these together with a robust reporting mechanism make way for an excellent user-experience. Every piece of activity data like the number of conversions, impressions and clicks should all be readily available. This makes evaluation of performance a cakewalk.

Efficient program management

In order to scale and run the affiliate programs in an efficient way, the merchants should be having dedicated affiliate managers. The role of the managers includes welcoming everyone with open arms so that these people can promote their products. But this procedure can only be made faster when the screening and approval of the affiliates is done in a timely manner and the affiliate managers make sure of that.

So, these are some of the criteria that you should check and keep in mind while you are selecting your affiliate marketing program.

Now, if you are still baffled as to where you can find all those high ticket affiliate programs, this list might just help you out.

- **BigCommerce** – With over 60,000 merchants, BigCommerce is definitely one of the well-known high-ticket affiliate programs in the world of e-commerce. Because of the presence of some advanced functionalities and numerous built-in features, BigCommerce is a real hit among the growing brands. One of the special features of this platform is that there is a provision for bounty payment amounting to 200% on the total price of the plan. Thus, the equivalent of this is that, you can $60, $250 or even $1500 at times for each paying customer. Apart from that, the cookie policy spans over a period of 90 days and you will get access to a weekly newsletter for affiliates that contain some of the latest SEO advice for you to implement.

- **Shopify** – Known as one of the most popular and advanced ecommerce website builders in the world, Shopify also has a very good affiliate program. They have over 400,000 merchants on their platform. The most profitable thing is that your conversion rates will automatically become boosted with Shopify because of their high reputation. Whenever an user signs up by clicking on your unique referral link, you will have the potential of earning $58 for each of those users.

Moreover, you can even get an amount of $2000 for every Plus referral and this sum is quite a good one.

- **3dcart** – This e-commerce platform is ever-growing and so is their affiliate program. Their generous commission structure is something every affiliate should check out because of their endless benefits. For every paid conversion, you can earn a commission of up to 300% and by joining their Partner program, you will have the potential to earn a separate 25% recurring commission too. Their affiliate managers are quite responsive and can help you out whenever you are stuck with something. To ensure access to a reliable third-party tracking, the website has teamed up with ShareaSale and Commission Junction. The platform has over 4000 affiliates working with them.

- **Volusion** – If you want to give a boost to your efforts in the e-commerce world, then Volusion can be your best friend. They are not only a highly advanced website builder but also have several responsive themes, payment gateways and inventory management. They also have tools that can help you with handling your client relationships, SEO marketing and email marketing campaigns. They use CJ affiliate to offer their affiliate program. With them, you can earn a one-time commission payment of 200% which is calculated on the client's hosting plan.

- **ClickFunnels** – This platform assists its users in creating a landing page that can assist people in creating marketing funnels. One of the most crucial aspects of a sales funnel is the landing page but they are not the only aspects of the entire funnel. There are a series of pages involved which ultimately make the customer convert and take their buying decision. They offer a recurring commission of 40% for every user. Apart from that, you also get another scope of earning when there are sales referred by those users whom you had referred in the first place. This is called sub-affiliate commission and this is of 5%.

- **Leadpages** – This is also a landing page builder and is widely known for its amazing affiliate program. Their landing page builder is of a drag-and-drop type that is of high utility to both Instagram and Facebook ad creators. Another important feature of this platform is their split testing tool and their ability to get seamlessly integrated with other marketing tools and applications on the web. They also have a rare feature, that is, there is a scope to earn commissions by sharing free content. They have some free short courses on their site and when you share the link of these courses with others and a customer signs up following that link which ultimately leads to a subscription, then you stand a chance of earning a commission. The recurring commission rate is 30%. You will also be able to host webinars together with them.

- **ManyChat** – This is a bot platform that will help the users manage their businesses in a seamless manner because of their sales, marketing and support services that you can use on Facebook Messenger. Integrating a bot in a business can definitely give it momentum by instantly increasing lead generation and sales. They also have a 100% commission rate.

- **Bluehost** – Well anyone who is interested in web hosting must have heard of Bluehost because of such high functionality and popularity. They have a variety of services like WordPress hosting, shared hosting, dedicated hosting and VPS hosting. They offer a flat fee or commission for every referral and it is an amount of $65. But you must know about a small yet considerable detail – you have to accumulate a sum of $100 before you can withdraw the commissions you have made. But on the bright side, they offer a cookie policy that stays for 90 days. Their customer tracking system is also advanced and this makes sure that you get your share of money for every referral you make.

- **Kinsta** – This is another of the platforms that offer services of managed WordPress hosting. Businesses which fall in the medium to large range are their main target customers and they have devised a special started plan for all of them. Apart from this they will also give you access to an extensive resource material that contains utilitarian content which is all about affiliate marketing. Their commissions range anywhere between $50 and $500 for every sale made and they also have a provision for 10% recurring commissions. They also offer other additional benefits like a 60-days cookie policy and a dashboard which is extremely user-friendly.

- **Cloudways** – This is another of the hosting services that are hugely popular. They provide a 24/7 expert support whereby you can solve all the queries you have. Their entire base of knowledge is quite extensive and they also have some of the best dedicated affiliate managers. They will also provide you with resources with which you can boost your affiliate marketing techniques. Their commissions are in the range of $50 to $125 for every sale made. The only drawback is the payout threshold which is quite high at $250. The audience targeted by Cloudways is mostly individuals and medium range businesses.

- **Liquid Web** – Known for providing data center solutions and managed web hosting solutions, Liquid Web is a company that is known for possessing a variety of partner programs. For commissions, you can earn anywhere between $100 and $1000 depending on a few factors and they will also give you recurring commissions. They have a 90-days cookie policy and send out special newsletters to affiliates on a quarterly basis. They also have referral programs which are specially made for IT consultants. You can also join their reseller program and get access to a tiered set of program discounts.

- **StudioPress** – This company is known for coming up with some of the major themes in the world. The Genesis Framework is their brainchild. More than half a million sites on WordPress ue the Genesis Framework as their theme. If you are someone who surfs the internet quite often, then you are bound to come across a website that has been built using the Genesis Framework theme. Although StudioPress is no longer a separate entity and has merged with WPEngine, no change has come to their individual affiliate programs and they are still separate. But you do need an approval to become their affiliate. The commission rate is quite handsome at 35% per sale made. They also have sub-affiliate commission rates of 5% and a 60-day cookie policy.

- **Template Monster** – This website too is responsible for providing different types of plugins and themes for WordPress along with other content management systems as well. They have a highly dedicated affiliate management team along with a 365-days cookie policy! For any first purchase, you can gain a commission of 30% and for all further purchases, a commission rate of 10% is set.

- **Udemy** – Being one of the most popular eCourse libraries, Udemy hosts courses on a variety of topics and has more than a million students under its umbrella already. They also have thousands of tutors on their platform who are teaching different skills. The website also offers discounted rates on some of the smaller training courses and students literally wait for such opportunities to come. You can earn a flat 20% commission for every sale and also get access to thousands of promotional material. But the only catch is that they have a 7-day cookie policy.

- **Coursera** – With over thousands of courses available on their platform, Coursera may not be as vast and extensive as Udemy but they definitely have their own fan base and their affiliate program is better too. Firstly, their commission rates vary from 20-40% for every sale made and most importantly, they offer a 30-days cookie policy which is obviously better than Udemy. Their affiliate program runs through Rakuten LinkShare. Their courses are also top-notch having some advanced content like quizzes and lectures that are framed after considerable research so as to provide the users with maximum knowledge.

- **Amazon** – The Amazon affiliate program is definitely the biggest but they do not provide hefty commissions. But with a proper strategy, you can make some good amount of money from Amazon affiliate program too. Their commission rates vary from 4% to 8.5% and they mostly depend on the total number of sales you made in a month. So, in order to increase your income margin, you will have to sell a lot of products or you can promote the high-ticket items on Amazon. Promoting high-ticket items is way easier and all you have to do is find the right audience who are really willing to buy those products. 4-8.5% of a high-ticket item is also quite a handsome amount of money and the best part is that there is no end to the variety of products on Amazon and so you have the full freedom to choose your niche.

So, these were some of the affiliate programs that have a considerably higher rate of commission than others in the market.

Chapter 7: How To Scale Up And Expand Your Business?

Three things are of utmost important if you want to become an affiliate marketing ninja and make a sustainable income out of it. These three things are – persistence, time and patience. Whatever you have learnt up till this point in this book will only get you started because the next most important thing that you are yet to learn is how you can scale up your campaigns and thus expand your affiliate marketing business.

This chapter talks about some of the most effective affiliate marketing strategies that you can implement in your business.

Don't scale too soon

This is something you need to learn even before you start scaling. If you do not scale your affiliate marketing campaign at the right time, you will never be able to realize the benefits you have been looking for. The problem with most people is that they lose patience and scale their campaigns way early in their affiliate marketing journey. When people are not willing to walk the extra mile, they will not be able to reap the benefits as well. The golden rule of scaling is that – a campaign that has a 75% ROI is much easier to scale than the one which is still at 25% ROI on a daily basis. So, you need to wait until your campaign is solid.

We have already discussed methods in previous chapters which will help you increase your profits but here is a recap of some of the easiest methods you can implement –

- Improve the audience you are targeting
- Think about better angles, ads and landing pages
- Pause the websites that are not bringing you any money
- Test offers

Pre-Scaling

So, if your campaign is not yet ready, it needs to undergo a process of pre-scaling whereby you will have to optimize it. Scaling requires resources and if your campaign failed just because it was not ready to be scaled, it will be a loss. So, in order to ensure that nothing goes to waste, you need to properly set up your campaign. Now you must be wondering what the difference between optimization and scaling is. Well, this is something everyone gets confused about. The difference lies in the gravity and size of the changes you are making. Optimization is all about the smaller changes and specific alterations that are done. Scaling is done after optimization is completed as this is the step you should take after having built a strong foundation in the form of a greater number of conversions.

So, here are some of the techniques of optimization that you should practice in order to make your campaign ready –

- Ensure that the campaign that you have designed runs equally well on mobiles and tablets, in other words, mobile responsive
- Adjust the call-to-actions or headlines or ad copies if and when needed
- The social media ad images should be changed if they are not grabbing enough attention or are performing poorly
- Don't invest everything on a single landing page and instead split test different landing pages

If this pre-scaling stage is followed properly, your campaign will automatically get a boost to reach the next stage faster. Once your campaign is ready, start scaling.

Increase your existing budget

This is the simplest of all the strategies mentioned in this chapter and well, this is something you all must have thought about. Investing more in what you are already doing is the first step towards scaling up your campaign. This is also quite a flexible strategy as it does not depend on the type of traffic source you have. So, with this strategy, all you need to focus on is figuring out what works best for you. If you find that your existing campaigns are bringing you a considerably sustainable amount of money, they why not scale them up by investing more? This will expand the reach of those campaigns much more. If you find that increasing the budget did the trick, you can allocate more funds later on so as to increase the performance of the same campaign even more.

But proper utilization of that increased budget is essential so that none of the money goes wasted. Here are some tips that you can keep in mind –

- Start off by increasing the budget of your Facebook ads. Facebook is the social platform that has the maximum number of users and so increasing your ad budget there will benefit you by increasing the potential reach.
- In case you are using search traffic, then try bidding on keywords that are more expensive.
- You should also invest more money in placing the ads at strategically better positions that are more prominent.

As you read about the rest of the strategies, you will find that most of them require you to spend more money in some way or the other but they also speak about some other considerable changes.

Acquire traffic from a different source

If you have found a campaign which, according to you is performing well, or a promotion angle that is offering more conversions, then you can attempt a traffic source transition in order to scale your campaign up. In simpler words, what you are trying to do is simply to replicate the aspects of that same success which you have seen with the hope that the same thing happens with you. Thus, you will be acquiring traffic in a way that will be different from what you were doing before. It's true that there is no guarantee of this working out but there is no harm in trying.

For example, suppose one of your campaigns on Adwords is doing really good. What you can do is try and run native ads and see the influx of traffic then. Are your Facebook ads bringing you some big numbers? Why not try the same type of ad on Twitter or Instagram? Yes, it might seem daunting but at times, it can actually work.

Expand your audience globally

Once of the greatest scaling opportunities is to gain traffic from multiple countries and not just one. But in order to dive into this strategy, you need to first build your stronghold in one country. Moreover, this is one of those strategies which can be tested rather easily. All you need to do is make a few tweaks here and there and adjust the parameters in order to make the new campaign. But the selection of the new country is very important. You need to select a country that is similar in some way to the country that you were already promoting in, that is, the country that was generating the conversions up till now. For example, if your preliminary campaigns were based in US, you can launch your campaigns in a country like Canada which is a lot similar to US. Firstly, both the countries have a majority of English-speaking audience. Secondly, due to the similarity in cultural altitudes and geographical proximity, both the countries have quite similar buying behaviors.

But, on the other hand, if your preliminary campaign was in the US, you cannot base your next audience to be in Japan. Both are completely different from each other and you will not get conversions. With time, you will understand the concept better and you will know which country pairs well with exactly which other country when it comes to campaign promotion.

Obtain a cap increase

Advertisers are the ones who set caps on the campaigns and this is done mainly due to the following two reasons –

- The advertisers usually set a specific budget for the campaigns and they do not usually want to exceed that allocated amount of money.

- They want to attract a high-quality traffic and not be flooded by too many leads.

Now, if the campaign that you have designed is running well and has managed to reach the cap way before than anticipated, this means that the quality of traffic that you are generating is high. At such situations, you can request for that cap to be raised on grounds that your campaign has the potential to earn more. But the quality of traffic you generate will play a huge role in the approval of increase of that cap. The advertiser would not be willing to make a cap increase if you are not providing leads that will actually bring in some revenue to the advertisers.

But in case you think you fit this criterion perfectly, all you need to do is contact your affiliate manager regarding the issue and then see whether he is willing to grant you the request of raising your cap.

Try to get a rate increase

This is rare but if you put your best foot forward, who knows you might be actually able to get your commission rate increased! But again this is only possible when your campaign is working extremely well and generating a lot of conversions, in other words, more revenue for the advertiser. Only then will the advertiser consider getting your rate increased because even he will want to gather more traffic. This will boost your ROI instantly. You can also get it done by contacting the affiliate manager. Although, don't bother taking all the stress if you are not generating quality traffic.

Capture emails of potential customers

A capture page can be used to collect the emails of potential customers. This is actually a part of long-term scaling strategies. This is also one of the ways in which you can churn out the full potential of a promotion you did for an offer. There are several services online which you can use and this will make a way for you to collect the emails of the users. The users will give their emails through an opt-in page.

You might be wondering what the goal of the strategy is. Well, your ultimate aim is to collect as many email addresses as you can of those users who were already interested in a specific niche. This will also help you construct a stable relationship with the user as you are providing them with an ongoing service and targeting them those product campaigns that they might show interest in.

Maintain your campaigns properly

This is one of the crucial steps that every affiliate marketer tends to miss out leading to a variety of problems. You should not deviate from your other campaigns in order to scale up one campaign. This means, you should not become so engrossed in one campaign that you forget to maintain the others. So, you should constantly be alert and keep testing new angles. This is important because what if the scaling doesn't work out? Then you will be left with nothing but loss. Don't let that happen. Don't ever betray your home base just because you want to expand.

Ensure proper cash flow

A proper and stable cash flow is crucial for the running of scaling campaigns. There is nothing worse than the inability to run a campaign just because you cannot fund it. But you must also not spend on your credit cards just because you need funds. This can easily lead to the formation of huge credit card debts.

If you are still unsure about scaling your affiliate marketing business, then think about it in the way of any traditional business, for example, a shoe store. If you are the owner and you find that you have made huge sales in this quarter, what would you do? Would you let things remain stagnant or would you make use of this perfect opportunity and boost the growth further? I would probably go with the latter option.

The most important lesson about an affiliate marketing business is that you have to treat it like a business. If you form your mindset then the path will become easier. Take the business approach and then let your mind brainstorm ideas for campaigns. The strategies mentioned in this chapter are some of the best ones you can use to scale your campaigns.

Chapter 8: Mistakes To Avoid With Affiliate Marketing

Everyone makes mistakes and so can affiliate marketers. But this chapter lists some of the most common mistakes which can be avoided if you learn about them. Mistakes are more common when you are just a beginner because that is the stage when you perform all the trial and error experiments with your campaigns and strategies. And that is exactly how you become a pro gradually. It is true that a mistake is what makes you wise but at times, these mistakes can be a costly affair and so are better off avoided. So, here are some of the common mistakes that every budding affiliate marketer is bound to make and the chapter also speaks about what you can do to prevent them.

Mistake 1 – Wrong product choice

Affiliate marketing campaigns cover every possible product on this plant and the product need not always be something physical. It can be digital too. But with so many options also comes the need to make the right choice. But can making the wrong choice impact your affiliate marketing strategy? Yes, it can. And so you need to be careful while selecting the product as this is one of your basic steps as an affiliate marketer. This can be your defining moment towards success, so don't rush it.

Your niche should be something that will drive you and inspire you to make good content. You shouldn't be forcing yourself to sit in front of your laptop and do research on products to promote. It should be your passion. When you are inspired from your niche, you can easily devise several other marketing strategies and activities around it. Moreover, the passion might take you to such a level that your work becomes even more authentic and unique and that is exactly what will help you to stand out from the rest of the affiliate marketers. A simple search on Google about ideas on affiliate marketing niches will bring you thousands of results but picking something randomly never works.

One very common mistake that several budding affiliate marketers make is choosing a niche just because it brings more money. You need to understand one very simple thing. No matter how prominent or cool the niche is, you will never be able to make it big if you yourself are not interested in it. Believe it or not, nobody in the world is a natural when it comes to affiliate marketer. Every big affiliate marketer of today started out with something they love and then they spent days and nights researching and sharpening their skills. But if the product choice is wrong, you will just feel like a slave doing this just for the sake of money and not because you really want to.

Mistake 2 – Promoting too many products right from the beginning

This is another mistake which people make but don't really see the fault in it. When you are just starting out in this field, there will be a temptation to include as many products as you can and start promoting all of them. Don't do that. The default approach towards affiliate marketing for any new person in this field is being over-enthusiastic and over-ambitious. But this will ultimately lead to stress and demotivation when you have to figure out proper strategies for all these products. You will quickly become less and less enthusiastic and drop the entire strategy altogether. It is easy to get distracted when you have too much on your plate and you will not have any time for yourself or for your family.

The value you are putting in starts lowering down and this, ultimately, brings down the number of sales. So, if you want to be smart, then focus less on the quantity and more on the quality because that is how you climb the ladder of success. Pick a handful of products which you personally feel good about and would love to promote. Research extensively on them and focus all your energy onto those products. When you commit your brainstorming capacity and focus on a single product at a time, you will come up with better ideas and statistics show that you will also find it easier to convert your promotions into actual sales.

If you are thinking that approaching affiliate marketing in this manner will do you no good and will only shun your growth then think again. There is no harm in proceeding one product at a time. Why cause havoc by trying your hand out at many things when you can make each product a success and then proceed? Every campaign is different from all aspects and thus, they need individual attention. So, you need to provide the campaigns with what they need and success is not far.

Mistake 3 – Only trying to sell and not help

With affiliate marketing, people often develop a mindset that is all about selling and not actually helping the audience with any information. If this continues, you will gradually start losing the audience that you have. Don't let sales become your only priority. Yes, you will have the tendency to do it, but remind yourself about long-term profitability. The mindset of making profits only will not give you poor results but also generate mediocre content. Good-quality content is what you should focus on. When your content is good, audience will follow and so will the sales.

Your writing should be focused on how the readers can benefit from it. Every feature should be explained in detail and think about all the probable questions that might pop up in the minds of the readers. Once you have figured the questions out, make a separate FAQ section with every piece of content and answer those questions there so that your audience is not left with any confusion. Keep friction at bay. The placement of banner ads can be sometimes frustrating to the audience. So place them accordingly so that they do not drive your readers so angry that they have reached a point of no-return.

Whenever you implement some sort of outbound sales tactic, some consequence will come. It is up to you to decide which ones you really want and which ones are not worth the hassle.

Mistake 4 – Poor quality website

This is another mistake that affiliate marketers make. Your content is definitely important but your content is not all about what you write. It is also about the platform. When your website quality is low, you will notice your traffic decreasing which results in a low volume of sales. If you are not an experienced web designer, don't worry because you don't have to be. No one is telling you to be perfect from the beginning. But with the resources that are available in today's world, making a good website is way easier than ever before. WordPress is one of the best places to start because of their user-friendly approach.

User experience matters a lot if you want to retain your audience. If there are too many ads on your webpage or if the page is not responsive enough, then your audience might simply migrate to some other page providing the same information. A messy template is also one of the many reasons which can scare off your visitors because your website might appear to be too complex for them. When you lose audience because of these cases, there are very low chances of gaining them back because no matter how much improvement you make, those people will remember your website for the bad experience they had.

You can understand this well when you compare it with shopping. Shoppers always prefer those shops which are clean and tidy and have everything arranged in a proper manner. They are even likely to spend more in such shops. But they will not visit an overcrowded mall because they cannot figure out anything over there. So, some of the things that you should make sure while building the website are –

- The website should be easily navigated
- Every section should be properly categorized and easy to find
- The website should be responsive

- The calls to action should be prominent and clear
- Every page should have only one call to action
- The on-site elements should be properly highlighted on the webpages and the design should be chosen accordingly

It's true that building a website can be overwhelming but when done with patience, it is not something impossible.

Mistake 5 – Content that is regular and of high-quality

Have you every though about what your product is as an affiliate marketer? Well, the answer is quite simple – it is your content. Every affiliate marketer wants to get more sales but in order to make your audience, you will first need to have good content. If readers find your content to be credible and valuable, they will automatically want to rely on your advice when they want to buy a product. The common misconception that almost every affiliate marketer has is that if you have 10 mediocre posts then it is equivalent to one great post. But this is a lie. It never happens that way.

No matter what type of content you produce, whether they are posts on product comparisons or product reviews, your sales will be directly or indirectly affected by the quality of your content. If your content is not actionable or insightful, then there is no use of publishing content at all. Consider yourself as the buyer every time you compose a new post and then think about the fact whether the post would have been useful to you or not. The universal rule of getting any person hooked to your writing is to make your content interesting.

The first step to composing a new post is to decide the topic. Once that is done, you need to research keywords. Find keywords that are relevant to your topic and have less competition. This has to be done if you want to outrank the competition that is already present. You should also check the word count of the posts that are ranking high on the first-page results. Then, set that word count as a benchmark for your own posts. Don't forget to include images in your posts because it is normally seen that posts with images automatically rank higher than posts that do not have any images at all. Lastly, be regular with your posts and don't make your audience wait too long for the next post.

Mistake 6 – Not keeping an eye on the performance of your website

Not making use of a tracking tool is another of the common mistakes made by affiliate marketers. You cannot simply have a glance at your website and say whether it is performing good or bad. You need to have access to advanced tools with which you can study the metrics. If you do not track your data, you will not be able to optimize it and without these two things marketing is simply nothing. Whatever strategies you are implementing or whatever tweaks you are making to your strategies or campaigns will have an effect and these tracking tools will help you study that effect. You need to be able to recognize all the patterns that are working out in your favor. Google Analytics is the best tool to monitor all aspects of the website performance but if you want, you can use any such similar tool as well.

Does your website have a good speed? This is another important aspect that is highly overlooked. Studies have proved that whenever a websites takes longer than 2 seconds to load, the audience bounce rate automatically increases by a whopping 50%. You have to keep it in mind that everyone is impatient. Everyone wants to see the content now or never. If you keep your audience waiting, they will simply find another site that won't be delaying them. Mode of content delivery, large file size and response times of the servers are some of the usual reasons of a slow website.

If you are facing problems with your file size, then you can use any of the online tools to compress your image. But you should keep in mind that the quality of the image should not be compromised. Taking these small steps can help you towards reducing the load time of your website.

Mistake 7 – Neglecting content readability

As already mentioned, readers are impatient. So, you have to take every measure possible to make your content user-friendly and readable. Whenever your content is hard to understand or the sentences are confusing, the tolerance level of your readers will start decreasing. The font size you use also matters. You need to choose the size that is not too big or too small. Avoid anything that is below 16pt. But the font size is not the only determining factor acting here. Your font style will matter too. Avoid fonts that are not clear. Moreover, prefer a serif font when it comes to constructing paragraphs.

Don't make your sentences long. Keep them short and crisp. A sentence should contain approximately 25 words because according to research, anything more than that becomes confusing to several people. Paragraphs should follow the same rules. Don't make them too long.

If you don't know the meaning of a word, then don't include it. An average reader prefers a grade eight or seven level of readability. Even those readers who have high academic qualifications prefer the readability level to the one mentioned before.

Mistake 8 – Ignoring SEO

Ignoring the basic aspects of SEO can definitely cost you a lot. If you do not include the proper meta descriptions and title tags, it will be impossible for people to find your content. And the sole motive of publishing these posts is to drive traffic so you should not forget SEO. The title tag should be compelling so that readers are bound to click on your post. If you are using WordPress, then the Yoast SEO plugin is a very good option to optimize your content and make it SEO-friendly.

To establish a proper hierarchy within your content, internal links are something you should implement.

Mistake 9 – Not making evergreen content

Something trendy comes up every other day on the internet and it can become difficult to keep up at times. But there will always be those topics which are evergreen and you should definitely include them on your website. Now, it is true that these topics have an immense amount of competition because everyone is writing on them. Moreover, they might also not be of much value to you as an affiliate.

But, when implemented correctly, these evergreen posts have high link building value. Sustainable content in the long-form layout can also be made more credible by adding phrases like '2019 updated edition' and your audience will automatically become interested in the updates.

If you think your content has any of the above-mentioned mistakes, then there is no harm in revising it again. Make the appropriate changes and then hit the Publish button.

Chapter 9: Strategies To Help Your Affiliate Links Outrun The Competition

The entire landscape of affiliate marketing has drastically changed over the past few years. Affiliates are now subjected to tighter legislations and thin content never does well with Google ranking. And top of all these things, the general competition has also increased by ten folds. So, if you truly want to get ahead of others in this game, you will have to play smart.

You need not be any expert to outrun others who are already established in this field. But what you need to do is push boundaries, give your best and follow the things mentioned in this chapter.

Strategy No. 1 – Stick to your niche

The number of niches that you can experiment with is plenty in number and the list is probably endless. But you need to focus on your own niche instead of trying to dominate over twenty. Yes, you will hear from others who maybe making millions from some niche which has just emerged. But does that mean you need to start doing that too? No. What you need to do is stick to your niche no matter what so that you can become an expert in that with time.

Moreover, when you juggle with so many niches at a time, you can never focus on any one of them. Deviating your focus to all the niches will only result in poor quality work. The result would be that you will have two dozens of niches and maybe each one has its own website but none of them will bring home a sustainable revenue.

This does not mean that you shouldn't experiment with the niches. Do as much experiment as you want but do not forego a niche just because you are not getting a quick success. Try your hand at a niche, do all that you can to make it boom and if even then you don't notice any growth, consider changing your niche.

Strategy No. 2 – Content is king

Your content will speak volumes about your work. If your content is solid, others will not be able to compete with it. You, as an affiliate marketer, are the middleman in the picture and so you also need to prove your value. For doing that, you need to come up with content ideas that others probably cannot compete with. Being an affiliate marketer has several advantages over brands that are already established. The first thing is that you have the opportunity to be agile and if you want, you can act instantly with your new content marketing strategies.

Make your content so good that others fall short of resources to even think about competing with it. Everything should be on point starting from the content itself to SEO, site speed, and even social media share-ability.

In today's world, you will find tons of affiliate marketers but when it comes to really testing or interacting with the products they promote, there are only a handful of marketers who do that. But the key strategy of developing your own dedicated audience is to grab their attention and provide value through your content. You need to provide details and some insights that are impossible for the consumer to gather all of his own. One of the best ways to do that is creating hands-on product comparison and review videos. You can also narrate anecdotes stating how that particular product fits like a glove into your daily life. This will make the audience believe that you are really acquainted with the product and with time, they will be ready to take your word for it.

Strategy 3 – Give some special bonus of your own

This is another strategy that can make you different from the thousands of affiliates out there and drive your audience to click on your affiliate links. You can sweeten the pot by giving your audience something extra. For example, one of the easiest ways to do this is by giving a special Facebook group access to those people who actually bought the product with your link. This group should have only those affiliates who had purchased the same product through your link.

You can also try rewarding those customers who have referred their friends. Word of mouth is something that will help you in spreading your business. Just get a plugin related to a customer referral program and you are all good to go. Now, your audience will then be able to share their unique link with their friends which will bring them to your website. And then you will earn from that extra portion of audience. But don't forget to reward your audience who promote you through their own links.

Strategy 4 – Practice hedging your strategies of SEO

This strategy is all about distributing your eggs and not keeping all of them in one basket. It is very similar to what happens in an investment portfolio. All of the money is not invested in any single entity. Instead, it is divided among bonds, stocks and other commodities so that your money remains safe through the ups and downs of the economy. Just like that, the Google algorithm undergoes some swings from time to time. Your SEO strategy has to be full-proof in order to survive these swings. The best way to do that is hedging your strategy properly.

First is the white hat strategy which is mostly effective for the long term. This will require the maximum amount of effort, time and money. During this strategy planning session, you will be focusing on a diverse range of topics at a time. But this strategy should be implemented on the main domain of the brand only. When it comes to short-term results, this is not the strategy you should be looking forward to. But in long-term, this is the safest bet you have got.

Second is the grey hat strategy which is purely made for acquiring medium term results. This strategy is all about setting up micro sites or buying other sites which are your competitors. The basis of this strategy is that tactics like widget links and guest blogging can be scaled to yield good results for the next 6-12 months but they won't be working after a period of 2-3 years.

Third is the black hat strategy or which is commonly known as the short term strategy. This approach is quite aggressive. The marketers buy hundreds of domains and then an extensive amount of link building is done which promotes these websites to higher ranks but that lasts only for a couple of weeks. To maintain that rank steadily, the entire process has to be repeated over and over again like a loop.

But if you want to make it big in your affiliate marketing business, then the best bet is to combine all the three strategies and form a multiple-layered diversification so that even if something fails, you always have a backup.

Strategy 5 – Practice out-branding, out-working and out-thinking

The competition is huge and so you have to give your best if you want to outrun that.

Out-branding. There are some underdog websites who have outrun the competition with a do or die attitude. This has been even more commonly seen in affiliate marketers who deal with credit cards and pay day loans. A simple search on Google would make it easier to understand for you. Use the keyword 'compare credit cards' and see which of the two sites rank 1st and 2nd. You will notice that both the companies listed are not any financial institution or bank. So, these companies have figures out a way to beat the competition they have with highly renowned banks and financial institutions that are focused on those same search terms as well.

Out-working. Every one of you must have heard about ProBlogger and Mashable. Yes, they are a success today but did you know that they were actually a one-man company when they just started. They out-hustled all the competitors they had. The same thing applies for those who are working in the field of affiliate marketing. It is not impossible to achieve that higher status or ranking in the Google search results but all you need is a more dedicated and solid strategy that can get you there. In case of Mashable, they used to publish as much as 7 blogs on a daily basis. That was way more than everyone else and fast forward a few years, Mashable ranks on the first page of Google whenever it is something in their niche. So, the endnote is that if you are into a niche that is over-competitive, you will have to possess the zeal that will make you work the extra hours.

Out-thinking. Last but not the least, you have to be smart. When you think smarter, you will always stay one step ahead of others working in the same niche.

Strategy 6 – Focus on building a recurring affiliate revenue

There is nothing that can be guaranteed when it comes to affiliate marketing. It is true that the market is extremely volatile and this is due to a variety of factors. The factors usually are case-sensitive and differ from one person to the other. For example, for Mr. X, it can be the Google algorithm that is not working in his favor while for Mr. Y, it can be because his main affiliate program is closing down.

But you need to be ready with a backup in order to face such unforeseen circumstances. What is the solution? You need to focus on recurring affiliate revenue generation. This will also keep you motivated while you are figuring out new ways to beat the competition. Of course, one-time payouts might seem good in an instance and there is no harm in them but with a recurring revenue, you are securing your own future.

Strategy 7 – Diversify

Many affiliates make the mistake of focusing all their energy and resources in one direction or one traffic source only. This mistake did cost a lot of affiliates their jobs back in 2011 when the initial Panda update of Google was released and thin or low-quality sites were pushed back in the search results.

Those who did not learn from their lesson faced a blow in their face again in 2012 when the Penguin update of Google was released. So, the safe lane to take is to build an audience that you own and build it by creating some high-quality content.

You can also diversify by focusing on different things. For example, maybe you were focusing only on one-word phrases as the keyword. Then it is time for you to concentrate on the long-tail keywords. According to research, these long-tail keywords are the ones that account for 70% of the searches on the web and are alone responsible for giving you a 36% conversion rate.

You can also try shifting your focus to a new demographic region or an audience that speaks a different language but only if it applies to the product you are promoting. You can also take into consideration the sales funnel and focus on different portions of it. For example, if you find that your competitors are more concentrated in building the top tier of the sales funnel, you can focus on strengthening the last tier which is located in close proximity to the call-to-action page.

With the market becoming ultra-competitive each passing day, these are only some of the strategies that can help you make it to the top. No one knows what will work best for you so you need to try your hand at everything. But don't make the mistake of trying out everything at once. Implement one strategy and then wait for the results. If it works then continue along that line and if it doesn't, start with something new. This list was meant to help you brainstorm your own ideas as well. Reaching the topmost rung in the ladder of success is not easy but it is not impossible if you are determined enough.

Chapter 10 (Bonus): An Action Plan To Kick-start Your Affiliate Marketing Business

If you have read all the previous chapters of this book, you must have formed quite a good idea about the various aspects of affiliate marketing and how everything works. So, this is a bonus chapter that lines out the exact steps you need to follow in order to kick-start your affiliate marketing business as a beginner. Everyone has to start somewhere but in order to get success, you need to do it the right way. Like any other undertaking, even affiliate marketing needs a plan and following that plan will bring you closer to your success.

Here is a step-by-step approach to affiliate marketing that will not only help you set up the business but also direct it towards the path of generating revenues.

Step 1 – Planning

The planning stage of setting up an affiliate marketing business is the most overwhelming but don't worry, you'll get past it. It is very normal to be tensed and feel like you are in the dark about everything. Relax! You are just starting out. But you need to do an extensive research to learn the basics and if you have read this book then you already know all that you need to know in order to start. The first thing that you should do is find the niche that you can work in. This is the first and foremost step because if you do not know what you are going to promote, you will not be able to figure out the audience let along build a website.

For starters, you can jot down all the things in life you are passionate about. You can become an affiliate of literally anything and everything. You should possess a certain interest in the field you want to start working with because when you love what you do, you will always stay motivated to work. Moreover, the niche you choose should not be shallow otherwise coming up with newer blog posts will become difficult for you as a beginner. You should also reconsider starting with a hugely popular niche for the simple reason that it is also going to have an immense competition to deal with.

Step 2 – Build your website

Once you are done with all that research, now it is time to put things into motion and build your own website. But wait! You also need to brainstorm a domain name. Every detail related to this has already been discussed in Chapter 3. But here I am going to discuss it in short. Well, unlike what most people think, building a website is not complicated especially with user-friendly platforms like WordPress, anyone can build a website. Once you have chosen a good domain name, buy it. The next step would be to choose a proper hosting plan. You can get quite affordable options in that too.

Now it is time for you to install WordPress. Choose a simple theme that is customizable and start creating content. Now, the content you put up on your website should not be anything random. It should be relatable to the audience and completely fall in your niche. Don't skip from one niche to the other every other month because your audience will then get confused. Master one niche and be an expert in that. Another important aspect of your content that you should keep in mind is that it should be engaging so that your readers don't lose their interest halfway through the post.

Step 3 – Choose your affiliate programs

Now it is time for you to choose the affiliate programs you want to work with and also select the products you will be promoting through your website. Now this is something you must have probably covered a bit when you were deciding your niche but now you have to dig deeper. Since this is something which will serve as the source of your income, you need to research extensively before you finally settle for a program. One of the most important things that you should definitely check while choosing the program is how much commission they are going to provide you per sale.

The affiliate program you choose should have products that you yourself would have personally used. If you don't believe in the products yourself, why promote them to others? If you continue such form of affiliate marketing you will never be able to gain credibility and trust of your audience. In order to become a success in this venture, you have to be as authentic as it can get. You should promote only those products which you think are trustworthy. You should also check how good the customer support of the affiliate program is and whether they have an affiliate manager or not. Suppose you have a problem regarding something, will they contact you instantly? You should choose a program that has prompt responses because you are bound to require support at some point of time.

Step 4 – Create high-quality content

As already said before, content is king. Creating good-quality content can be time-consuming indeed but it will also pay you off well in the future. So, you need to have patience and start building new posts in your niche regularly. One of the most common models of content is writing product reviews. When it comes to generating a sustainable amount of affiliate income, product reviews can go a long way to help you out. The best example of this type of content model is *The Wire Cutter*.

You can also try constructing blog posts that revolve around some common day-to-day problems that people face and what products they can use to overcome those problems. Research various forums on the web to know about the things people are now talking about. Pick the topics that are relevant to your niche, do some keyword research and then construct the blog post.

Another way of creating an information website is to put in some evergreen posts that literally serve as a knowledge hub. These posts are all about information that never ages. But before you plan an evergreen content, the most important part is to do proper keyword research.

Giving some type of informational product to your readers is another way of attracting traffic. This can be anything like an e-book or a webinar. The goal is to set up the base for email marketing. When your audience signs up for the free stuff, they provide you with their email address which you can then use for promoting your affiliate products.

Step 5 – Build your own audience

This is something that goes hand-in-hand with quality content production. When your content resonates with the audience, you will automatically find traffic flocking in. When an audience is literally interested in what you post, they will also be more inclined towards making a purchase. And this is what you need to make revenues.

Social media is one of the easiest ways in which you can build an audience for yourself. There are so many social media platforms to choose from – Facebook, Instagram, Twitter and Pinterest. There are other networks too which are often location-specific. If you are just a beginner, then you can also start by writing guest posts for other websites which have already gained a considerable amount of popularity and rank way higher in Google search results. This will give you exposure to the audience who might be willing to read posts in your niche.

Another important way that you should implement is by building an email list. Form a lead magnet by providing your audience with some informational product and then you can use that magnet to gather the email addresses. Don't push sleazy sales pitches but instead create some useful content that the audience might be actually interested in. Through those content pieces, you can direct the audience towards your website whereby they can click on your affiliate links to make the purchase.

And in between all these, don't forget the SEO strategies as they are the ones which will help your posts reach the right audience group.

Step 6 – Implement analytics

Analytics are an important part of achieving success in the scope of affiliate marketing. So, you need to set up your Google Analytics account. When you learn about the details of the traffic data, you will be able to point out exactly what type of ad copy is performing well when it comes to converting an audience. The data that Google Analytics provides the users is vast. Yes, it can seem a bit complicated at first but with time, you will find it easier. Every piece of information that you gain from the insights of Google Analytics can help you to increase audience conversion if proper tactics are used.

You can know literally everything about your audience. You can find out the geographic location they are coming from or even the device they are using to browse. You can also find out the times of the day when your website is attracting the maximum amount of traffic. Geolocation is one of the most useful strategic metric that you can implement to increase traffic and sales both. When you know the geolocation of your audience, you can customize your ad copies or emails accordingly. You can also think about other aligned locations to promote your data in because of the similarity in buying habits of the people belonging to the two locations.

Step 7 – Ensure profitability

You also need to ensure profitability if you want to continue on your affiliate marketing strategy. Well, you might not be able to see any income in the initial months but with time, you will see sales coming in. But with that gradual rise, there will also come a point where your income will become stagnant and there will be no further growth. But you should not allow that to happen. Keep maximizing your profits.

But for starters, if you do not want to spend more than you earn, start with a few products only. The more the number of products, the more overwhelming it can become for you. Test different campaign strategies and don't go all in with just one. With gradual testing, you will understand what is actually working out for you. There is another important factor that people often tend to overlook – demand. If you are trying to promote a product that doesn't have that much demand in the market, you will never see good results.

So, you need to listen to the market. The market will give you signs regarding what you should do and all you need to do is look out for them and respond accordingly. Being a highly competitive field, there are several new updates that keep cropping up and you need to watch out for everything new so as to stay in the loop.

Step 8 – Maximize your performance level

To churn out the full potential of your affiliate marketing campaign, at some point or the other, you will have to optimize it. You should also focus more on the landing pages that you are building. They are the ones to grab your audience's attention. Firstly, you will have to understand your audience, know exactly what they want and then construct the landing pages accordingly. Customize your pages from time to time so as to make them suitable for the audience you have.

You can also consider giving some extra incentives that will drive your audience into converting. These extra incentives can be anything from free trials and exclusive discount rates to freebies or anything that is free. Keep testing and you will find the perfect fit for your growth.

Step 9 – Scale up

When you scale up your affiliate marketing strategy or campaign, you do it to bring in more profits. But first you have to deal with the budget concern. You need to ensure that you have the right amount of cash flow before you start scaling up your campaign. Don't ever think about meeting the costs using your credit card. That is a bad practice and can easily line up debts.

One of the first steps that you can take in order to vertically scale your campaign is to increase your daily budget. But your ROI should be solid. You need to remember that every campaign in the world of affiliate marketing has the potential to be scaled but every campaign has its own time. If you do not scale your campaign at the right time, you won't be able to see the results you were expecting. This means, you should not scale your campaign too early or too late.

Another important strategy of scaling that you can use is by expanding your global reach. Research which countries align in culture and buying habits with the country you are currently promoting in. Then, include that other country (with similar metrics) under your target umbrella. This way you can bring in a completely new set of traffic to your website.

Every detail related to scaling has been discussed in Chapter 7 in case you want more information.

Step 10 – Automate

All the strategies and steps that you have learnt so far are definitely strenuous and involve a lot of work on your part. And you definitely need to perform all of this manually so that you can learn it all. But later on, when your business booms and reaches a certain success level, you will have too much on your plate and you will have to implement automation for most processes.

The first thing that you should automate is email-marketing. This strategy has the potential to generate a lot of sales when implemented in the right manner. The next thing that you need to handle is segregating your leads. This can also be automated with the help of different platforms that you can find through a simple Google search.

One of the strategies to grow your affiliate marketing business is to be active on social media and then promote your posts there. But this need not be done manually as you can easily automate them.

When you create so much content for your website, it also means you have to do that much amount of proofreading. But with technology becoming advanced day-by-day, you don't really have to do that. One of the best tools that you can use for proofreading is Grammarly. It is very easy to use and it can check all the grammar errors and spelling mistakes that are present in your post.

Over the past few years, automation technology has taken a completely new face and thanks to that, affiliate marketers can now go on expanding their business without having to worry about hiring any more personnel. Now you need to adjust your budget and ROI accordingly because all these automation processes won't come for free.

So, if you are someone who is willing to dive into the world of affiliate marketing, this 10-step action plan is just custom made for you. Follow it step-by-step and you are sure to reach your goals soon enough.

Conclusion

When you have read the complete book, you will develop a total grasp on the concept of affiliate marketing. By now, you should be all ready and geared up to start your own business. If you keep thinking and rethinking, you will never be able to start and *now* will always be the best time to start.

With affiliate marketing, you will be in charge of all the decisions as you will be working for yourself and not anyone else. The main effort is to set up your strategies and content. The phases that come later on are mostly about reaping the benefits and some tweaks here and there. The key benefit of being an affiliate marketer is that you are not actually making any of the products, you are only selling them.

But even affiliate marketing is all about the audience and so you have to do everything you can to keep your audience satisfied and provide some actual value through your content. If you create something that is already present on the internet, why will the audience come to you? The goal is to be unique and authentic. Your posts should have your personal touch that no one can replicate.

You can also try creating videos to make the content even more enticing and immersive. Who doesn't love the idea of making money while you are enjoying your vacation or sipping your coffee? With affiliate marketing, you can make that dream come true.

Lastly, if you find this book helpful in any way, don't forget to leave a review on Amazon.

www.ingramcontent.com/pod-product-compliance
Lightning Source LLC
Chambersburg PA
CBHW070837070326
40690CB00009B/1586